NOT-FOR-PARENTS

ROME

Everything you ever wanted to know

Klay Lamprell

CONTENTS

I WISH I'D DRESSED MORE WARMLY

JUNO WHO I AM?

DON'T MAKE ME YOUR DINNER

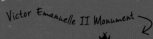

The Colosseum

The Forum

Victor Emanuelle II Monument

NOT-FOR-PARENTS

THIS IS NOT A GUIDEBOOK. And it is definitely Not-for-parents.

IT IS THE REAL INSIDE STORY about one of the world's most famous cities – Rome. In this book you'll hear fascinating tales about **ancient gladiators** and modern footballers, crazy traffic, yummy food and **gruesome** history.

Check out cool stories about fighting with **wild animals**, spooky stone statues, drag racing Roman style and lucky fountains. You'll find zippy motor scooters, **fashion freaks**, some seriously ancient bridges and **ice cream** flavours galore.

This book shows you a **ROME** your parents probably don't even know about.

GLAD TO BE A GLADIATOR...NOT

Slaves, criminals, and prisoners-of-war could be chosen for gladiator school. The upside was three meals a day and a chance at the big-time. The downside was death. Even if you survived a few bouts in the ring at the Colosseum, the years of tough training and the injuries along the way would probably kill you by the age of thirty.

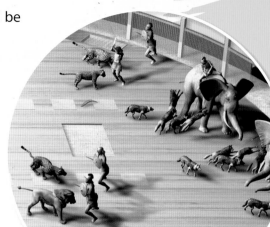

CHOOSE YOUR WEAPON

There were about 30 types of gladiator, and they all used different weapons, shields, and armor. Swords were common, but there were also deadly three-pronged forks known as tridents, long spears, and even strong nets that were thrown over opponents.

Trident

Leg protector

Shoulder guard

Shield

Club

Sword

How beastly!
Specialist gladiators battled lions, tigers, crocodiles, and even elephants. Other times criminals had to fight animals to the death, or creatures were forced to attack each other.

Star power
Gladiators were the sports stars of Rome, and the best ones were very famous, like Spartacus the rebel slave, Marcus Attilius, and Flamma of Syria. Even the emperors Commodus and Caligula couldn't resist fighting in the arena.

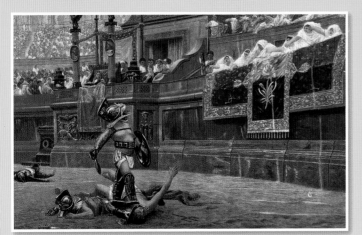

Crowd control

When a gladiator was injured or surrendered, the crowd decided his fate. If they thought he had fought well, they raised their thumbs to let him live. If it was thumbs down, he was to be killed.

> I SURE AM GLAD I HAVE ALL THIS ARMOR!

Make a killing

Because gladiators were expensive to feed and train, they weren't allowed to die in battle unless the sponsor of the fight paid a lot of money to the trainer. The more deaths in a day of fights, the more generous the host was said to be.

WANT MORE?

The Colosseum—www.archeoroma.beniculturali.it/en

FATHER FIGURES

While legend has it that the twins were raised by a shepherd, some say their real dad was the god of war, Mars. Others claim it was the hero Hercules.

WHY ROME ISN'T REME

Once upon a time there were twin boys called Romulus and Remus who were dumped at birth. A wolf found them and raised them for a bit until a shepherd became their dad. When they grew up the boys had a fight over where to build a city, and Romulus killed Remus. That could be why Rome isn't Reme.

"WOLF" WOULD BE A MUCH BETTER NAME FOR A CITY...

Sibling rivalry

The boys started building their own cities on different hills. Remus came over to check out how his brother was going, and laughed at the low city walls, so Romulus killed him!

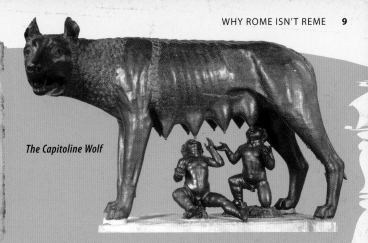

SMALL BITES

✫ The twins' mum was a priestess.

✫ The boys were put into a basket and floated off on the Tiber River.

✫ A woodpecker helped the wolf feed them.

✫ Romulus started his city on Palatine Hill.

✫ Remus preferred Aventine Hill.

The Capitoline Wolf

Howl old is it?

People thought the famous bronze Capitoline Wolf statue had been around for thousands of years, perhaps since the fifth century BC. Then scientists took a close look and worked out that it was only sculpted about 800 years ago.

The wolf is the emblem of the A.S. Roma soccer club.

What's in a name?

The last real Roman emperor was also called Romulus. In fact his full name, Romulus Augustus, combines those of the city's founder and of Rome's first emperor, Augustus. The reign of Romulus Augustus lasted for less than a year, and its end marked the fall of ancient Rome.

All in together

The style of the earliest Roman house was a very simple circular hut with a thatched roof, central pole, and a hearth in the middle.

WANT MORE?

Museum of Roman Civilization—en.museociviltaromana.it

ALL ROADS LEAD TO ROME

The Romans realized that without good roads they weren't going to get very far in their effort to conquer the world. The Via Appia was their first go at a solid, paved road that could handle the heavy traffic of large armies. It went from Rome to Brindisi, which was a port town. From there the Romans could take ships to Egypt, Greece and North Africa. Having a road like this gave them much greater power, so they nicknamed the road Regina Viarum, meaning Queen of Roads.

All roads lead to...
Via Appia was the first of a network of roads that covered over 75,000 miles (120,000km). The saying "all roads lead to Rome" came about because during the Roman Empire, all roads really did lead to Rome!

The Via Appia took heavy loads.

A TOUGH ROAD

Before Via Appia, roads were basically dirt tracks. It took clever thinking and a whole lot of slavepower to build a road that could bear the weight of marching armies, wheeled wagons with heavy loads, and the hooves of horses, mules, and oxen. As well, it had to survive blazing dry heat and regular rain.

Via Appia today

Though it was built in 312 BC, the course of the Via Appia can still be seen, and some parts of the road are so intact you can walk on the original paving!

Digging the base...

...to create a stable road.

Milestones marked the distance.

DESIGNED TO LAST

★ Romans built drainage into the road.
★ They used local resources, paving the road with *basoli*—slabs cut from the hardened lava of nearby volcanoes.
★ The paving slabs were cut into polygonal (many-sided) shapes so they could be laid out like a jigsaw puzzle, which locked in the pieces.
★ Signposts, called *miliarium*, marked out each Roman mile, which was a distance of about 0.9 miles (1.5km).

WANT MORE?

Via Appia Regional Park—www.parcoappiaantica.it/en

RELIGIOUS HABITS

People who work for religious organizations often wear uniforms. Roman Catholic nuns and sisters wear uniforms called habits. There are many different groups within the Catholic Church called orders, and each order has its own habit.

Papal tiara

Father fashionista
In the 16th century Pope Pius V refused to wear the luxurious red robes worn by previous popes and chose instead simple white. To this day popes wear white.

Brigidine

Franciscan

ON PARADE

An order's habit depends on which saint the order is devoted to and the kind of work the order does. Some orders these days don't wear special clothing, but in Rome habits are still on parade!

Redemptoristine

"NO ONE TOLD ME I HAD TO WEAR THIS..."

Earning their stripes

The guards who protect the pope have worn the colors of the powerful Medici family since Giovanni di Lorenzo de' Medici became Pope Leo X in 1513.

Habit-forming

Every Wednesday and Sunday, nuns from various orders come to St. Peter's Square in Vatican City (which is really more like a circle) to join the general public in receiving a blessing from the pope.

Missionary of Charity

Try keeping this clean!

Carmelite

Missionary of Mary Help of Christians

WANT MORE?

Lots of habits—www.nunsandsisters.com

What a view!
The president of Italy sees this ancient Roman obelisk when he looks out from the Quirinal Palace.

From the pharaohs
The obelisk in the Piazza della Rotonda was originally erected at Heliopolis in Egypt by the pharaoh Ramses II over 3,000 years ago!

SEEN ONE COLUMN...

You might think if you've seen one column you've seen them all. But every column tells a story of a time, a person, a place, or an event in history. There's a special type of column called an obelisk, and Rome has more of them than any city in the world—some ancient, some modern, all pretty impressive!

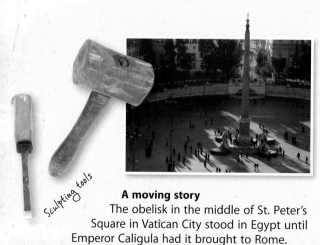

Sculpting tools

A moving story
The obelisk in the middle of St. Peter's Square in Vatican City stood in Egypt until Emperor Caligula had it brought to Rome.

Granite giant
The Agonalis obelisk was originally built for the emperor Domitian. Now it sits on top of a fountain in the Piazza Navona.

A HANDFUL OF HISTORY

The ancient Romans were so into Egyptian monuments that they built massive ships to carry obelisks from the city of Alexandria over the Mediterranean Sea to Rome. Then they used monstrous cranes to put them up around the city.

A marble marvel
Trajan's Column, which is an impressive 115ft (35m) high, was built to celebrate two successful wars waged by the emperor Trajan.

Stories in stone
The 2,500 figures that are carved into the column tell the story of Rome's victories over the Dacians.

Piazza del Popolo

Tuthmosis obelisk

Santa Maria sopra Minerva

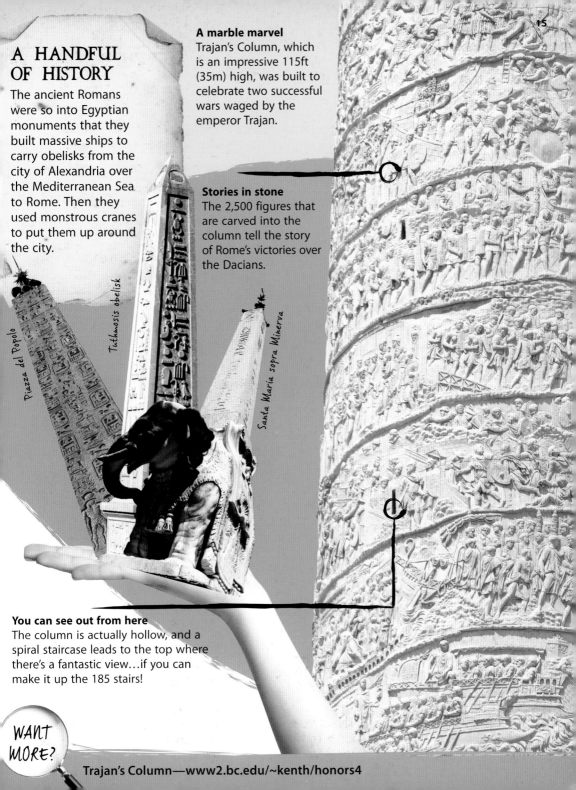

You can see out from here
The column is actually hollow, and a spiral staircase leads to the top where there's a fantastic view…if you can make it up the 185 stairs!

WANT MORE?

Trajan's Column—www2.bc.edu/~kenth/honors4

ANYONE FOR CAPPUCIN-OH?

What do monks and cappuccinos have to do with each other? Cappuccino foam is a sort of hood on top of hot coffee, like the hoods worn by the Capuchin monks. But that's not all that makes these monks famous. The walls and ceilings of their crypt in Rome are decorated with the bones of 4,000 Capuchin monks who died between 1500 and 1870. Some of the skeletons still wear their robes!

FROTHY FRIARS

The monks got the name Capuchin from wearing a hood called a *cappuccio*. In Italian if you add "-ino" to the end of a word you make it mean "small" so cappucc+ino is a small hood. Think about that next time you see someone sipping on a frothy coffee...

Monk business
The Capuchin monks follow the example of Saint Francis, who lived a simple life about 800 years ago, spending all his time helping out the sick and the poor.

I THINK I'M STUCK IN A RUT

Dressed to kill
Capuchin monks are known not only for their hoods, but also their long beards. (Only the live ones wear beards!)

Skeleton staff
The monks spend time around the crypt's bony decorations to remind themselves of how fleeting human life is.

Cheery thought
A sign in the crypt reads: "What you are now, we once were; what we are now, you shall be."

UNDERGROUND SCENE

The crypt of the Capuchin monks is underneath a church called the Santa Maria della Concezione. It is divided into several sections, one of which features a skull with wings made of shoulder blades attached to it. There is also a Crypt of the Pelvises and a Crypt of the Leg Bones and Thigh Bones—creepy!

WANT MORE?

The Capuchin's website—www.cappucciniviaveneto.it/cappuccini_ing.html

VATICAN

Set within high walls inside Rome is the world's smallest state, owned by the Catholic Church and run by the pope. Only about 800 people actually live inside the Vatican, including the pope whose house is the Apostolic Palace.

Burning ambition
When a pope dies, some cardinals hold a secret vote to decide which of them will take over the job. If the election is successful, the ballot papers are burned with chemicals to produce white smoke. If not, they are burned to produce black smoke.

Where do we go from here?
There have been 21 Ecumenical Councils of the Catholic Church. The last one, held almost 50 years ago, discussed the direction of the church.

First-glass travel
The current pope is German, so his favorite form of transportation is a Mercedes-Benz "Popemobile," which has a glass room for him in the back.

CITY KEYS

The Vatican's coat of arms features two keys that have been the symbols of the Holy See for centuries. The gold key represents Heaven, the silver one represents the pope.

Growing interest

The design of the papal coat of arms was inspired by the colorful trees and hedges in a garden near the Vatican's central administration building. Nearly half of the Vatican's land area contains gardens that have been there since medieval times. Most have fountains and sculptures, and there's even a heliport for the pope.

OVER FOUR MILLION PEOPLE COME TO VISIT EVERY YEAR!

Tiny city, big See
Vatican City is the smallest state in the world and has only existed since 1929. But the Holy See—which is like the government of the Catholic Church—has been around for almost 2,000 years.

WANT MORE?

The official Vatican website—www.vaticanstate.va

With an oink, oink here...
There are some strange gatherings of creatures great and small in Rome each year when people bring all sorts of pets and farmyard animals to be given a blessing by a priest. The patron saint of animals, Saint Anthony the Abbot, is also the protector of butchers!

THE PET SET

If you're a cat in Rome, you've got it made. You're protected by law and even if you're homeless, you're sure to be fed by your local restaurant or one of the cat-loving women called *gattare* who make it their job to care for stray cats. Dogs do pretty well too. They are welcome in stores and restaurants, and even have their own special dog-parking spots!

Dogs of war

Ancient Romans had armies of aggressive dogs that they would send into battle hungry and armed with heavily spiked collars. They first used a breed called Molossian until they went to Britain and discovered a more powerful type of dog called Pugnaces Britanniae.

PICTURE THIS

Many postcards of Rome feature cats of all shapes, sizes, and colors perched on cars, sleeping amid ruins, and snuggled into statues. Why? Because that's really how it is in Rome! For over 20 years it's been illegal to kill stray cats, so colonies of feral felines live throughout the city.

THESE PEOPLE ARE MY BFFS...

Safe haven

Largo di Torre Argentina, a square in Rome that houses the ruins of the Theatre of Pompey where Emperor Julius Caesar was stabbed to death, is now a cat sanctuary. It is run by volunteers who feed and care for up to 300 stray, abandoned, and wounded kittens and cats.

WANT MORE?

The Cat Sanctuary—www.knowyourcat.info/getcat/catsinrome.htm

FASHION FEST

From old-school cool and trendy Fendi, to togas and T-shirts, looking good has always been important to Romans. Fabrics, fashions, and fads have come and gone over the centuries, but one thing has never changed—a local wouldn't dream of walking out their door without throwing on a stylish outfit.

Fashion that flatters
From the dudettes and dudes in denim riding scooters and hanging around the piazza to moms and dads in dresses or suits heading to work or out for dinner, Romans dress their best.

Paint the town red
Men in ancient Rome wore togas with red borders during festivals, while women wore tunics with blue borders.

Get it white!
Roman men at formal events wore plain white togas. It was an important occasion when a boy wore his first white toga.

A special shade
Important people such as generals, judges, and emperors wore purple togas decorated with gold.

It's in the bag
Roman women are famously fashionable, and one thing they choose with utmost care is their handbag—you'll see all shapes and sizes of bag, but they'll always match the outfit!

Fit for a funeral
While some emperors wore black togas, they were usually the choice of people who were mourning the death of someone close.

Emperor

Plebeian

Slave

Senator

Equestrian

Strap them on...

The ancient Romans wore light leather sandals around the home. Heavy sandals were used by soldiers or gladiators. Modern versions of Roman sandals are now worn by fashion lovers around the world.

VIA DEI CONDOTTI R.IV

Wrap it up

Only Roman citizens were allowed to wear togas, but they didn't always want to. Woolen togas could be hot and difficult to put on and keep on. This is why Romans jumped into their lighter, shorter, and more comfortable tunics whenever they could.

All robes lead to Rome

The center of Roman fashion is a stylish stretch of road known as Via Condotti. Via Veneto is also a favorite with the chic crowd.

WANT MORE?

Roman clothing in detail—www.roman-colosseum.info/roman-clothing

PIAZZA NAVONA R.VI
(STADIO DI DOMIZIANO)

Get 'em hot!
When the weather turns cold in Rome Piazza Navona is a hotspot for roasted chestnuts. They taste a bit like sweet roast potato.

Piazza Navona began life as a sports venue with room for 30,000 spectators. It was built by Emperor Domitian and given the clever name Domitian's Stadium. Now it's a buzzing city square—a favorite meeting place for locals, and a workplace for artists and street entertainers.

WATER WAY TO SPEND THE DAY!

Swimming in the square
The ancient stadium went to ruin but was revived in the 17th century by Pope Innocent X, who ordered that every weekend in the hottest month of August the piazza should be flooded to create a waterpark for wealthy Romans.

GOOD SEATS

Domitian's Stadium, also known as Circus Agonalis, was used mostly for footraces and other athletics. Occasionally it was flooded so that mock naval games could be held. Audiences had good seats everywhere in Circus Agonalis because the seating sloped from 13ft (4m) at the arena edge to a height of 100ft (30m) at the outer perimeter.

DON'T HIT THE BIRDS...DON'T HIT THE BIRDS...

Staying in shape
Domitian built his stadium around 2,000 years ago. The stadium is long gone but its shape is plain to see today. The square itself is where the athletes once competed, while the buildings around the square are where the spectators sat.

The footprint of Domitian's Stadium.

ACTION STATIONS

Busking is big business in Piazza Navona. Along with the "statues"— people painted white, silver, or gold who make money from not moving a muscle—there's the action of jugglers, clowns, hip musicians rocking out on electric guitars and saxophones, and dancers with seriously cool moves.

What's in a name?
"Navona" might come from the name of the games held there— the Agonal games. *In agone* could have gone to *n'agone* to *navone* then *navona*. Or Navona might be from *naumachia*, the Roman word for the place where naval battles were re-enacted.

WANT MORE?

KEEPING CLEAN

Imagine going to the toilet with 300 to 1,500 of your closest friends! That's how it was done in ancient Rome. Bathing and going to the toilet were done in public at your local bathhouse, which also had a gym, a swimming pool, spa and sauna, and a restaurant or two. You might have chatted with friends, conducted business, or even met your future husband or wife at a bathhouse.

MIXED MESSAGES

Bathhouses had three entrances —one for men, one for women, and one for slaves. Men and women were allowed to bathe together in some places, but mostly they visited at different times of the day. Children weren't allowed in at all— so does that mean Roman kids never had to have baths?

Too much information!
Sounds gross, but the Romans went to the toilet in public. Even more gross, a sponge on a stick was used instead of toilet paper. Water running beneath them carried their waste away.

Danger below!
Only the nobles and rich middle classes had toilets at home, or could afford to go to the toilets at the public baths. Ordinary folk used pots that they then emptied into vats. If the vats were full, they'd tip the contents out into the street!

A HANDFUL OF HISTORY

★ There were hot and cold baths and steam rooms.

★ Slaves kept log fires alight to heat the water.

★ Professional masseurs would rub scented oil into visitors' skin.

★ At one time there were around 900 baths in Rome.

The local hangout

Multistory buildings attached to bathhouses were often decorated with mosaics and statues, and contained anything from libraries and lecture theaters to fashion shops and stages for singers and jugglers.

Cool colonnades

Rows of high columns joined together at the top were called colonnades. They often surrounded the open-air sections of the bathhouse where people would go swimming or do their exercise routines. These areas could also be used for wrestling, ball games, and even weightlifting and boxing.

WANT MORE?

Water and sewerage in ancient Rome—www.waterhistory.org/histories/rome

Mint condition

Most images of the Colosseum that remain from Roman times are on old coins. Some commemorate its opening in AD 80, and others celebrate its restoration 150 years later.

SCHOOL OF HARD KNOCKS

Criminals were often punished by being sent to gladiator school. They usually ended up dying in a one-on-one duel or as part of a group slaughtered in the arena. Slaves were sometimes sent to gladiator school, too, and could win their freedom if they fought well.

Seats for senators

NOTE TO SELF: WEAR MORE ARMOR NEXT TIME...

COLOSSAL KILLING SPREE

For its grand opening alone, over 5,000 animals and as many people were killed at the Colosseum. Wild elephants and lions brought from Africa were hunted down as entertainment. Bears were starved for days and then let loose among unarmed people. Gladiators fought to the death, and the arena was filled with water for violent naval battles.

Celebrations for the opening of the Colosseum ran for 100 days.

Roman numerals

Capacity	50,000	Trapdoors in arena	36
Entrances	80	Animal pens	32
Height	164ft (50m)	Building time	8 years

Cheap seats

Emperor's seat

Expandable roof

I MAY HAVE A CAPE, BUT I DON'T HAVE ANY SUPER POWERS.

Holding cells

Guards

Crowd control
Roman legionary soldiers made sure spectators didn't cause trouble.

THE BIG TIME

The Colosseum was named after a statue of Emperor Nero—called the Colossus Neronis—that was 98ft (30m) high. Colossal means gigantic, and the Colosseum sure fit the bill—it was the largest amphitheater in the Roman Empire!

WANT MORE?

The Colosseum—www.archeoroma.beniculturali.it/en/

WHAT TRASH!

In the oldest parts of Rome where the streets are paved, fast food wrappers and cigarette butts stare up at you from between the cobblestones. In the outer areas, the trash lines the streets. But then leaving litter is an ancient Roman custom. Ancient Romans would dump their trash in piles in the streets or even throw it out their windows. There are still mounds that remain to this day that are mainly made up of broken bits of pottery.

BURNING ISSUE

Most journeys made by Romans are by car, and in a city as big as Rome that means serious air pollution. Things weren't much better back in ancient Rome, with the amount of smoke from cooking, burning trash, and workshops often making the air dangerous to breathe.

Holy light

The Vatican has committed itself to becoming one of the world's first carbon-neutral states, installing solar panels and a solar generator. It even has plans to build a solar power plant.

Roman rats love their trash

In 2010, environmental campaigners built a hotel in Rome out of trash found on the beaches of Europe.

A growing problem

The trash piles used to get so big that the Romans would build roads or even houses on top of them! As the piles got higher, the level of the streets rose and more stones were needed to keep the city above its own garbage.

Rome sweep Rome...

WANT MORE?

Romans and tourists generate 5,000 tons of waste every day.

Do you see what eye see?

Trompe l'oeil is an artistic technique sometimes called illusionism that is all about deceiving the viewer. It's like the first type of 3D movie! The name means "trick the eye" in French, but some of the best examples of this technique can be found in Rome.

TRICKING THE EYE

Magicians play tricks on our eyes when they make an object appear out of thin air, or disappear into nothingness. Some artists play similar tricks when they make it seem that buildings are bigger or smaller, rounder or flatter, farther away or closer than they actually are.

PALACE OF ILLUSIONS

The Palazzo Spada is a palace that isn't always what it seems. A gallery off the central courtyard is built with a rising floor and shrinking columns. This makes the gallery look more than four times its actual length and a tiny sculpture at the end look life-sized!

SOME PERSPECTIVE

☆ The *trompe l'oeil* passage is almost 500 years old.

☆ It was the work of artist Francesco Borromini.

☆ A mathematician helped with the design.

CAN SOMEBODY PLEASE SCRATCH MY NOSE?

WATCH THE MOUTH!

The artists and architects behind the city's many optical illusions should beware La Bocca della Verita, or the Mouth of Truth. Legend has it that this ancient marble sculpture will bite off the hand of any liar foolish enough to put an arm in its mouth.

Key to the city

Look through the keyhole in a door at the Villa Malta for the city's best view of the dome of St. Peter's Basilica. It looks great framed by trees and a garden path.

Things are looking up!

That's the inside of a dome...isn't it? Actually it's another *trompe-l'oeil* illusion painted on a flat part of the ceiling of the Church of St. Ignatius.

WANT MORE?

Trompe l'oeil examples—www.architecture.about.com/od/graffiti/g/trompe.htm

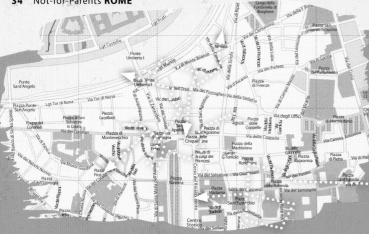

Simple names

Some streets were named for trades. Around the marketplace of Campo dei Fiori there is Via dei Cappellari—the road of the hatters—and Via dei Chiavari—the road of the key-makers.

ADDRESS-LESS

We can't imagine living without an address but in Rome, only a few major streets had names—generally the names of the wealthy people or the politicians who paid for the street to be built. Instead, Romans just described where they lived. Can you imagine what the post office would do with this address: the house five steps from the temple of Pomponius at the point where the trees bend over the fountain on the earthed road with the gravel surface...

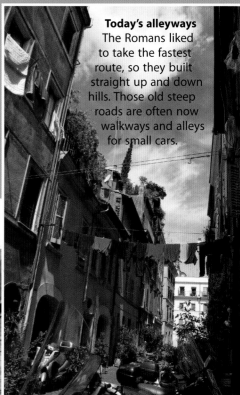

Today's alleyways

The Romans liked to take the fastest route, so they built straight up and down hills. Those old steep roads are often now walkways and alleys for small cars.

Pedestrian access only

Vehicles weren't allowed on roads inside the city walls during the day. Not everyone walked though—wealthy women were carried on "litters" by slaves.

HANDFUL OF HISTORY

✯ An address was basically a description.

✯ Some streets were privately owned.

✯ There was a private and a public postal system.

✯ Most smaller roads were leveled earth.

✯ In Italian, a road is a *via,* or if it is small, it is a *viale.*

Ancient highway
The Via Sacra, meaning Sacred Way, was Rome's widest road and the main highway through the Forum.

> I'M SURE THERE WAS A CAFE SOMEWHERE ALONG HERE...

> Almost 2,000 years after they were built, many Roman roads are still used.

> YOU CAN CALL ME AURELIUS THE MARVELOUS.

THE GOOD GUYS

Roman emperors were not only military leaders, priests, and lawmakers but also had responsibility for the basic structures of an efficient society, like water and roads. In the era of the "Five good emperors" —Nerva, Trajan, Hadrian, Antonius Pius, and Marcus Aurelius—much attention was given to building and repairing roads. Good roads were a major factor in the success of the Roman empire.

WANT MORE?

A searchable street map of Rome—www.rome.info/map

CAVES OF THE CATACOMBS

Beneath the ground around Rome is a network of spooky tunnels called catacombs, where Jews and Christians buried thousands of their dead in ancient times. Hundreds of miles long, the walls of the catacombs are lined with tombs that sometimes hold more than one body. Most of the caves are closed but there are a few that can be toured, only with a guide. Try not to get lost!

WILL DANCE FOR FOOD! WE'RE NOTHING BUT BONES.

Can you dig it?

The volcanic rock beneath Rome is perfect for digging tunnels—it's soft until it's exposed to air, then it becomes hard and strong. Which is lucky because the Christians and Jews, who were usually poor and often slaves, had nowhere else to bury their dead.

A FIRST FOR FRESCOES

The Catacomb of Commodilla contains one of the first images of Jesus Christ with a beard. Before this image was created almost 400 years after his birth, Jesus was usually shown as a young barefaced shepherd. The symbols beside his head are the first and last letters of the Greek alphabet and symbolize the phrase, "I am the beginning and the end."

Underground scene

The dark, dry catacombs are the best place in the world to see early Christian art. There are different styles of painting created over hundreds of years, with highlights including a picture of the prophet Jonah being thrown into the sea and several Adam and Eve images (complete with fig leaves).

ARCH RIVALS

★ There are some elaborate marble tombs with arches known as *arcosolia* in the catacombs.

★ The "Greek Chapel" in the Catacombs of Priscilla has an arch covered in frescoes of Biblical scenes.

★ Many martyr tombs were converted into chapels, often with great arched entrances.

WANT MORE? Official website—www.catacombe.roma.it

DRAG RACING ROMAN STYLE

The Circus Maximus is not a big tent with clowns and high-wire acts. It was a racetrack for chariot racing, a very cool—and freakily dangerous—sport in ancient Rome. Around the track was seating for 250,000 fans. That's almost double any sports stadium today! Now it's just an empty field with the occasional jogger.

A HANDFUL OF HISTORY

* A chariot was pulled by two, often four, horses.

* Sometimes camels and ostriches replaced horses.

* Elephants once broke through the barriers protecting the crowd.

* The winner received palms, crowns, and cash.

Silent circus
The area is mostly quiet now, but Circus Maximus can still draw a crowd. Almost three quarters of a million Romans celebrated there when Italy won the soccer World Cup in 2006.

The color of money

Wealthy people got together to buy horses and chariots, and organize betting on the races. There were green, blue, red, and white teams, and the chariot drivers wore tunics in these colors so that the crowd could follow the action and cheer on their chosen charioteers.

NERO AT THE REIGN

As a special treat for the crowds, six or seven horses would be put at the helm. If this wasn't tricky enough to manage, in the time of Emperor Nero sometimes 10 horses were used to draw a chariot.

A fatal turn

The most dangerous part of a race was when the chariots had to turn at the end of the straight. Sometimes crashes were accidental, sometimes not!

I SHOULD HAVE GONE TO THE BATHROOM BEFORE THE RACE...

WANT MORE?

After the races there was free food at the exits to encourage the crowds to GO HOME!

RESTING PLACES

While Christians were buried in the catacombs, non-Christians were buried in graves, mausoleums, and *columbaria*. A mausoleum is an aboveground burial tomb. A *columbarium* is an underground place where urns containing ashes of the dead are stored. The term *columbarium* comes from the Latin word for dove—because these burial chambers had holes in the walls for the urns, they looked like dovecotes.

The pyramid tomb

Sculpture of sadness
The Angel of Grief sculpture in Rome's Protestant Cemetery was created over 100 years ago by American sculptor William Wetmore Story for the gravestone of his wife.

WHEN I'M DONE COUNTING TO 100 YOU ALL BETTER HAVE GOOD HIDING SPOTS!

Niche market
Many Romans would pay "rent" to a *columbarium* to save a spot for their ashes. They would sometimes buy a memorial plaque or even a sculpture of their head to place with their mortal remains.

HISTORY IN THE HEADSTONES

In the Protestant Cemetery, well-fed cats wander the graves of famous artists, writers, and scientists who died while visiting Rome or who had made the city their home. Next door is an ancient pyramid built as a tomb for a wealthy judge. Explorers broke into the tomb in 1660, but they weren't the first people to visit. Everything inside had been plundered long ago.

Cecilia's cemetery
Wealthy and important people were generally buried in circular mausoleums. Like the Egyptian pyramids, the dead were placed in a room deep inside. The tomb for a woman named Cecilia Metella is one of the best examples of burial buildings from ancient Rome.

Baker's delight
The baker Eurysaces was obviously proud of his trade. His tomb is built in the shape of an oven. Pictures showing the various stages of bread production run along the top.

WANT MORE?

The bodies of poor Romans were simply placed in a casket and thrown into a river.

FLOWERS AND FIRE

Before it was paved, Piazza Campo dei Fiori was an empty meadow used by the army for military practice. It then became the site of a horse market and also a gallows where people were tortured and executed. Pope Sixtus IV had the place cleaned up so it could become a thoroughfare for pilgrims heading to the Vatican, and the open-air food markets moved here.

Flooding and flowers
The area now covered by the piazza wasn't developed until the 1400s partly because it was so close to the river and often flooded. This made the soil rich food for flowers.

Giordano Bruno

Daily deliveries
For over 140 years, stalls selling fresh food, flowers, and knickknacks have filled the piazza six mornings a week.

Arancio
clementine

Limone

Rosa

NOT SO SWEET...

Though it has a sweet name—"field of flowers" in English—some gruesome events occurred here. The statue in Campo dei Fiori is of philosopher Giordano Bruno who was accused of being a heretic, meaning he had crazy ideas like Earth moves around the Sun. He was burned alive here in 1600.

Frutta

Carciofo

Arancio Siciliano

ROSA CANINA 0,50€ UNO

Meeting and eating
The stalls disappear in the early afternoon and by evening the cafés, shops, bars, and restaurants are in full swing. The piazza is a cool spot for locals and tourists to meet and eat.

DUH! YOU CAN BURN ME BUT YOU CAN'T BURN MY IDEAS...

During the inquisition, many people died in the same way...

WANT MORE?

360° panorama—www.360cities.net/image/campo-de-fiori

PORT OF ROME

Wild animals for the games at the Colosseum as well as food, trinkets, and building materials came by ship into the port of Ostia and were taken along the Tiber River to Rome. In time the river changed direction and Ostia was buried in soil that preserved it. Being a few thousand years old it's a little crumbly now, but you can see how it would have been.

FORT TO PORT

Ostia first attracted settlers because it was near salt flats. Salt was important to ancient Romans because it kept meat from rotting. Rome's early rulers built a big fort at Ostia to stop invaders before they could travel inland. As Rome's empire expanded, the town outgrew the fort and Ostia became a thriving port city.

Beasts of burden
Paintings and tiled mosaics show that camels and elephants were used to transport goods around Ostia. The bones they left behind show signs that they were not treated very well.

WILD RUMPUS

Wild animals from every corner of the empire were a major attraction for Romans. Roars of angry leopards, lions, and tigers, alongside the screeches of panicked monkeys and the trumpeting of frightened elephants, echoed across the waters as boats arrived into Ostia. The furious sounds of the caged beasts advertised the thrilling entertainment to come at the Colosseum.

Keep 'em coming
To keep Colosseum audiences and private collectors happy, hunters looked for new animals to bring to Rome. Zebras, giraffes, hippopotamus, camels, rhinoceros, and even crocodiles were unloaded at Ostia.

TRADE CENTRAL

Ostia was one big marketplace. Sell, sell, sell and buy, buy, buy! Traders from all parts of the empire mixed with local merchants and officials, networking at the baths and doing deals at the forum.

Potted history

Clay containers, called *amphoras*, were used to transport oil, wine, olives, and other foods. *Amphoras* washed up on shore from old shipwrecks help historians work out how far the Romans traveled.

On the waterfront

To move caged beasts and giant chunks of marble from the ships to the shore, the Romans used pulleys and cranes manually operated by slaves and elephants.

WHAT WAS IMPORTED

✳ grain ✳ marble
✳ wine ✳ oil
✳ animals

WANT MORE?

CUPID

His name comes from "cupido," which is Latin for desire. Cupid was a boy with wings, the son of Venus who was the goddess of love and beauty. A person struck by the arrows from his bow would fall in love.

Diana, goddess of nature and hunting
All things wild, natural, and pure were Diana's realm, so she was not only goddess of hunting but also of the moon, fertility, and childbirth. She was also patron of slaves.

EVERYDAY GODS

The ancient Romans worshipped a huge number of gods and goddesses. Each one looked after a particular aspect of nature and everyday life. Some had big responsibilities, like hunting, war, weather, and wisdom. Others looked after little tasks, like cooking, cleaning, and opening the door to your house. The symbols for these gods and goddesses are all over Rome.

SYMBOLS OF POWER

Gods and goddesses had symbols that represented their specific powers. As king of all gods, Jupiter's symbol was a thunderbolt. Themis, the goddess of justice, was represented in a set of scales. Bees were the tiny messengers of the gods.

Juno, queen of the gods
As protector of the Roman empire, Juno was known as Regina, meaning queen. Her main temple was close to the mint because she looked after money.

STREET SHRINES

The Roman gods have been a little bit neglected lately, but there are plenty of reminders of Christian faith around the city. This is a shrine to the Virgin Mary.

Neptune, god of the sea
The trident carried by Neptune resembles an ancient three-pronged fishing spear. It was a symbol of power, used by Neptune to attract lightning, stir up water, and cause earthquakes. He is also known as Neptune Equester, the god of horses and horse racing.

Mercury, god of trade
As the caretaker of trade, travel, and profit, Mercury needed to move swiftly. He wore winged sandals and a winged hat.

Minerva, goddess of wisdom
Minerva was an all-rounder. Not only was she the goddess of wisdom but also of medicine, the arts, science, trade, and war. She invented numbers and musical instruments.

Mars, god of war
At first Mars was the god of spring, so he looked after growth in nature, fertility, and cattle. In time he became a god of death and eventually the god of war.

WANT MORE?

The gods Janus, Mars, Maia, and Juno have months named after them.

THE SEVEN HILLS–COUNT 'EM!

Before there was Rome, there were small groups of people living on the seven hills. They started out having the occasional get-together, and before long they were one big happy neighborhood. They drained the muddy valleys between the hills, started some markets there, and Rome came into being. It certainly wasn't built in a day.

What's in a name?
They are called the seven hills but in reality most were high ridges, separated by marshes.

I Quirinal
The highest of the seven hills is the site of the Palazzo del Quirinale, the official home of the President of Italy.

Caelian
Archeologists digging around the Baths of Caracalla—the place where Romans cleaned themselves, went to the toilet, and hung out with friends—have found remains of luxury homes, showing this was once a very wealthy area.

IV

II Viminal
The smallest of the hills and the last to be included inside the walls of Rome is now the site of the city's main train station, Termini.

III Capitoline
It once housed a temple to Jupiter, king of all gods. Now it's best known as the site of buildings and courtyards designed by Michelangelo (though he died before they were completed). Capitol Hill in Washington DC, in the USA, is named after this hill.

The seven hills

WORTHY OF MENTION...

Though it isn't one of *the* seven hills of Rome, Pincian Hill—the Hill of Gardens—is within the city walls and it's important to modern Rome as the site of the Borghese villa, gardens, and museums.

DON'T TELL THE SECRET!

Janiculum

This hill is sometimes mistaken for one of the original hills of Rome, but it's not! It is high though, so there are good views over Rome. There's also a huge statue of military hero Giuseppe Garibaldi, who helped bring the different parts of Italy together into one unified country.

Esquiline

VI

One end of Esquiline was once used for dumping garbage and burying the poor in pits. Now it's best known as the site of Emperor Nero's "golden house" and the church of Santa Maria Maggiore.

Palatine

VII

According to legend, this is where Romulus came when he decided to build Rome. Wealthy Romans built their grand homes here because it was so close to the Forum and had nice views. The ruins of emperors' palaces make Palatine Hill an open-air museum.

Aventine

V

This wealthy area has a magic spot! In a piazza just past an orange orchard on the Via di Santa Sabina there is a heavy, green door with a keyhole that looks right through to St. Peter's dome.

WANT MORE?

Palatine Hill was home to Rome's rich and powerful. "Palatine" gave us the word palace.

BRILLIANT BUILDERS

For thousands of years people have tried to work out how the massive Pantheon has survived. We would be hard pressed today to create a similar structure. The Pantheon is the largest unreinforced concrete dome in the world.

Famous residents
The Pantheon is also a tomb! Kings, painters, composers, and architects are buried here.

BEING BURIED HERE ROCKS!

Dome of the Pantheon
The Pantheon is most famous for its roof. It's so big that the walls holding it up had to be made of concrete 20ft (6m) thick!

BUILT, REBUILT, AND BUILT AGAIN

The Pantheon has been built three times. The first two burned down, but this one has survived for almost 2,000 years. Originally the Pantheon was dedicated to all gods, but since it was given to the pope in 609, the Pantheon has been used as a Catholic church.

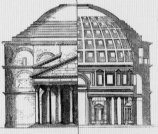

Early Pantheon

Pantheon since 120 BC

Not your average temple

From the outside the Pantheon looks like most Greek temples, with eight huge columns out the front. But inside it's huge! It's 140ft (43m) across and up!

HOLY

There's a hole in the center of the dome, called an *oculus*. It's 26ft (8m) wide, and it's the only way that light comes into the building. The shaft of light it casts is always slowly moving.

Tough stuff

We know Romans invented concrete, making it out of volcanic ash, lime, and rock, but no one knows exactly what was in the concrete used to create the staying power of the Pantheon.

Drainage holes

Rainwater that falls through the *oculus* is drained off through little holes in the floor. Clever!

WANT MORE?

The Pantheon—www.italyguides.it/us/roma/pantheon.htm

Keeping the inheritance

The Colosseum is proof of the ancient Roman genius for design and construction. It's survived plenty of earthquakes, years of scavenging, trampling by tourists, plus pollution and vibrations from traffic. It's been around for 2,000 years, but can we continue to preserve it?

IT'S IN RUINS

As ancient cities go, Rome is one of the more expressive. Its history hangs out in its ruins for everyone to see. And there's plenty more to see where that came from. Dig a deep hole in Rome, and you're likely to find an ancient bit of something or other!

The Forum as it is

As the Forum fell apart, bits of the buildings were taken to be used elsewhere and the site became a dump. The ground level rose and the place was buried. It was only a hundred years ago that the big work began on uncovering the ruins.

READING THE RUINS

Archeologists—the people who study the ruins of ancient places to uncover history—have a field day in Rome. But it can be slow going. An archeologist's job is also to keep ruins safe and protect what they find, so they have to sift through everything ever so carefully...

GREAT, MORE DIRT.

Workers digging Rome's new subway line have to stop each time they bump into something old and interesting.

The Forum as it was
Anything big that happened in Rome happened at the Forum. It was trade central, a hotspot for politics, and the heart of religious life.

WANT MORE?

360º view of the Forum today—www.arounder.eu/fori/lucaemartinafullscreen.mov

WATER WONDER

The Trevi Fountain is a sculpture of a god in a big shell being pulled along by two seahorses that are being driven by two tritons (messengers of the sea). Throwing coins into the pool below the fountain is thought to bring you back to Rome, especially if you throw with your right hand over your left shoulder.

I'M THIRSTY

What's in a name?
In Italian, *tre vie* means three roads, so the name of the fountain has to do with the three roads that come together at the busy Piazza di Trevi.

WHO'S WHO OF THE TREVI

Trevi Fountain was commissioned by Pope Clement XII and designed by sculptor Nicola Salvi. Work started in 1732 and many artists helped during the 30 years it took to complete. Salvi died before it was finished. The statue's main man is Neptune, who is god of the sea and of horses.

For a good cause
Every week thousands of euros are collected from the fountain and given to the charity Caritas, who use the money to buy food and clothes for people in need.

Caritas

WANT MORE?

Piazza di Trevi ☆ The Trevi Fountain—www.trevifountain.net

WORK IT!

Italian scientific inventions and designs are behind many everyday objects, like eyeglasses, batteries, coffee machines, and the telephone. The ancient, Romans were big on inventions of equipment, too, like the weapons they developed that helped them take over other cities and create their empire!

LOTS A VOLTS

We measure electricity in "volts" because it was Alessandro Volta who created the first electrical batteries. They were known as voltaic piles because they were stacks of metal disks held in place by glass rods.

I'M HAVING A SHOCKING DAY!

Espresso
In 1901, Luigi Bezzera changed coffee-making forever by inventing a machine that could make individual cups of coffee real fast using hot steam.

Nitroglycerin
In 1846, chemist Ascanio Sobrero created nitroglycerin, which we still use to stop chest pain and to blow things up!

Battery
Alessandro Volta discovered that putting certain metals together created electrical energy. Thanks to him, we now have batteries!

SIEGE WEAPONS

Ancient cities were walled to protect the citizens from attack. The ancient Romans invented weapons that could catapult missiles over the walls and also help get them inside. This was the start of modern warfare.

Telephone

In 1871, Italian Antonio Meucci invented a device for voice communication. Scotsman Alexander Bell brought the telephone to the world.

Eyeglasses

Salvino D'Armate is said to have invented the first wearable eyeglasses way back in 1284.

Thermometer

Santorio Santorio built the first device that accurately measures temperature—a thermometer.

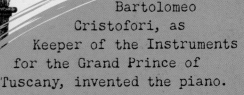

Bartolomeo Cristofori, as Keeper of the Instruments for the Grand Prince of Tuscany, invented the piano.

WANT MORE?

Explora Museum in Rome—www.mdbr.it

SPOOKY STONES

What do you do if you think someone isn't telling you the truth? Take them to the Mouth of Truth, or Bocca della Verita as the Romans call it. Legend has it that the mouth will bite off the hand of anyone who is telling a lie!

MMM...TASTES LIKE CHICKEN

OWIE!

Truth be told
It's thought that the Mouth of Truth sculpture was part of a fountain or was perhaps even an ancient drain cover. It was put in the Church of Santa Maria in Cosmedin 500 years ago and is now a major tourist attraction.

Magic door
This ancient "alchemical gate" stands in a park near Rome's main train station. The story goes that if you can interpret the mysterious inscriptions around the door you'll be able to pass through to the great unknown.

The guys on guard are images of Bes, an Egyptian god...

SAY IT ON A STATUE

A few hundred years ago, when it was illegal to speak out against the government or church, people would sneak out at night and hang their written comments on sculptures in the busiest parts of town. They soon became known as the talking statues.

THEY CALL ME PASQUINO!

I'M MARPHORUS!

I'M MADAME LUCRETIA!

I'M IL BABBUINO!

Fame with a name
The Romans were fond of their talking statues and gave them nicknames. The first was Pasquino, who is still a poster boy for freedom of expression. Others included Friar Luigi and Babbuino—the baboon.

WANT MORE?

Bocca della Verita official website—www.dpsusa.com/bocca_verita_history.shtml

WALK THE SCRATCHED STREETS

Many of Rome's ancient walls are covered in spray paint, some of it just scribbles and some of it elaborate works of art. There are campaigns to clean it up, but there also people who like it because it puts art into the streets for all to see, instead of keeping it inside museums, galleries, and churches. So is it vandalism or valid art? What do you think?

The writing on the wall
No wall in Rome is safe from posters promoting political parties or the next big band to play in town.

GRAFFITI IS THE ITALIAN WORD FOR SCRATCHES. SCRATCHED GRAFFITI WAS MADE IN ANCIENT TIMES.

Legal art
Rome offers artists plenty of opportunities to legally show their works, from annual festivals like "100 painters of Via Margutta" to daily displays in Piazza Navona and at the top of the Spanish Steps. So what drives street artists?

Art at heart
Many of Rome's street artists are serious about their craft, and some are classically trained. Chalk artists re-create famous paintings in exchange for tips from tourists.

THIS IS MY FAVORITE SUIT

In fashion?

VIA R.XIII DELL'ARCO DI S CALISTO

Hot coffee?

Stencils and paste-ups
Stencil graffiti works by spraying paint over a design cut out of cardboard. It's fast and can be done over and over again. Paste-ups are printed on paper and then pasted to a wall.

Sticky situation

Express yourself!
Whether in words or pictures, people have been using public places to tell stories, make comments, and generally express themselves for thousands of years. It's illegal, as it is in most places, to put your own designs on Rome's walls and pavements without permission, but with spray paint and marker pens, it's fast and easy to get away with.

WANT MORE?

Aufidius was here. Graffiti has changed little in 2,000 years, except possibly the names.

MARVELOUS MOSAICS

Churches aren't just for praying in. They're also for decorating. Artists have had a field day with Santa Maria Maggiore, using real gold in the walls, making crazy patterns on the floors, creating action scenes using tiny mosaic tiles, and sculpting marble to look like real people. You don't have to know much about religion or art—they're pretty much in your face!

A fresh face
The core of the church was built over 1,500 year ago and has changed little since. The outside i almost brand new—not even 300 years old!

LET ME GIVE YOU A SKETCH

Pope Liberius in design mode
The church is dedicated to Mary, the mother of Jesus. It was called Santa Maria Maggiore, meaning St. Mary Major, because it is the biggest of the churches devoted to her.

ST. MARY OF THE SNOW

According to legend, one night in AD 358 Pope Liberius was visited in his dreams by the Virgin Mary. She told him that he must build a new church and that the correct spot would be marked by snow the next day. Sure enough, in the morning there was snow on top of Esquiline Hill, even though it was the middle of summer.

SNOW DOME

The miraculous snowy origin of the church is commemorated every year on August 5. There isn't much snow about in summer, so instead, white flower petals are scattered from the dome.

Wall-to-wall drama
Before television, you could count on a church mosaic for a hefty bit of drama. Tiny tiles of colored marble and gold were put together to tell stories.

WANT MORE?

See inside—www.panoramas.dk/fullscreen/fullscreen46.html

SPOT OF SPORT

There's only one thing Romans love more than their food, and that's soccer. *Il calcio*, as it's known in Italy (from *calciare*, meaning *to kick*), is a national religion. Roma and Lazio are two big teams in Rome that play in the country's top division, Serie A. Locals don't choose a team—their family does that for them at birth. The rise and fall of their team's fortunes often has a great influence on a Roman's life.

Simply marble-lous!l
The Foro Italico is the city's main sports complex. Its Stadio Olimpico is the home ground for both Roma and Lazio. It also contains the Stadio dei Marmi with its many marble statues of athletes.

THE WOLVES

The yellow and red (*Giallorossi*) half of Rome follows Associazione Sportiva Roma. Founded in 1927, Roma are three-times Italian champions, last time in the 2000–01 season. The club's symbol is a she-wolf with the two baby brothers Romulus and Remus who feature in the myth of the creation of Rome.

THE EAGLES

The white and sky-blue (*Biancocelesti*) half of Rome follows Società Sportiva Lazio. Founded in 1900, Lazio are twice Italian champions, last time in the 1999–2000 season. The club's symbol is the eagle, which harks back to the emblem (known as the *aquila*) that the Roman army once carried into battle.

Big boots
Professional soccer players such as Roma striker Jeremy Menez and Lazio striker Mauro Zárate are worshipped like gods in Rome.

True colors
Fanatical fans known as "ultras" sing songs, wave banners, and light flares at most matches, but the excitement really ramps up when Roma plays Lazio.

WANT MORE?

Soccer in Rome—www.italyheaven.co.uk/rome/football.html

Ancient Roman flamingo feast
Flamingo tongues and stuffed flamingos made a dinner party special. Romans also liked an element of surprise—what looked like roast pig might turn out to be dessert.

FOOD FUN

The truth about who first made pasta is as mixed up as a plate of spaghetti. These days, though, you say pasta and everyone thinks Italy. Ditto pizza. Roman soldiers baked pizza on their shields. Maybe that's why pizza in Rome has a thin crust with a small amount of bubbling-hot, fresh topping.

Tripe

Saltimbocca veal

Pick your fork
Rome has a long tradition of eating the innards of cows. They call it *quinto quarto*, meaning the fifth quarter. Recipes use the tail, the intestines, and the stomach lining, called tripe. Veal meat, from very young cows, is often prepared *saltimbocca*, meaning "jump into the mouth" (that's how good it tastes). And when it comes to using chilies, Romans make a sauce *arrabbiat* It means "angry!"

Pasta

Every area of Italy has its own special pasta dishes. In Rome, common pastas are *bucatini* and *tonnarelli*. Both are like spaghetti, but *bucatini* is thicker with a hole through the center while *tonnarelli* is more square. Pasta sauces are often made with *guanciale*—pig's cheek—and *pecorino* cheese.

Fish sauce

Liquamen, a salty sauce made from fermented fish guts, was as common as ketchup in ancient Rome and was made in big factories.

Everyone loves pizza

Since Roman pizzas have a thin crust and light toppings, you can order a whole pizza for yourself at a restaurant. Takeout places, called *pizza al taglio* or *pizza rustica*, have squares of freshly made pizza on display. You choose how much you want and pay by the weight.

WANT MORE?

Liquamen recipe—www.coquinaria.nl/english/recipes/garum.htm

THE JEWISH QUARTER

In 1555, Pope Paul IV decided that Jewish people in Rome had to move into a small, walled area, called a ghetto. The gates of the ghetto were locked at night. If they left the ghetto by day, Jews had to wear a yellow patch so they could be recognized. It was 300 years before Jews were given equal rights of citizenship and the ghetto was closed down.

A HANDFUL OF HISTORY

* ✱ A separate language developed in the ghetto.
* ✱ Forced to attend Catholic mass, Jews used earplugs!
* ✱ Jewish doctors could not treat Christians.
* ✱ Children were sometimes kidnapped and converted.
* ✱ Jews paid for guards who locked them in at night!

Ghetto gastronomy
In the ghetto food was hard to get. Deep frying added flavor and kept stomachs full for longer. Artichokes were easy to get, and are served even now Jewish style in Rome—deep fried then flattened and fried again to make the leaves crisp. Yum!

Kosher Rome
Because it's been home for so long to a large Jewish community, a lot of the food that is typical of Rome, like salt cod, fried zucchini flowers, and ricotta desserts, is *kosher*—it meets Jewish dietary laws.

OLD-SCHOOL GHETTO

The Great Synagogue, which is the main place of worship for Jews in Rome, was built after the ghetto was closed. It's hard to miss. It is a tall building and its squared dome makes it different from other places of worship.

Then

At first around 3,000 people were in the ghetto with just a single fountain for fresh water. By the time the ghetto was closed, thousands more lived there in tall, cramped apartment blocks with limited light and air. Dark and dirty about sums it up.

Now

Today the ghetto neighborhood is a social hot spot, a food-lover's paradise, and a center of artistic life. There are no walls and gates, or signs that say "ghetto," but you can tell when you're entering the ancient Jewish quarter from the store signs in Hebrew and the six-pointed Jewish symbol, the Star of David, in windows.

WANT MORE?

The Great Synagogue—www.sacred-destinations.com/italy/rome-great-synagogue

Arch of Septimius

Built in white marble, this was a welcome home tribute to Emperor Septimius Severus, who had been away conquering Parthia.

WHERE'S MY FACE?

Castel Sant'Angelo—emperors' tomb

Emperor Hadrian began building this in AD 123 as a burial chamber for himself and his family. Emperor Antoninus Pius finished it 16 years later, and the ashes of all emperors were put here for the next hundred years.

REMEMBER ME!

When one is very important, one likes a massive monument to make everyone remember who one was and what one did. Rome is dotted with these tributes, some ancient and in ruins, some modern and imposing.

MONUMENT OR MONSTROSITY?

Built for Victor Emanuel II —first king of modern Italy—this big structure has a few nicknames, including white elephant, typewriter, and wedding cake. Romans like the view from the top because from there you can't see the monument!

A HARD ACT

If you were an actor in olden days Rome, your best bet was to perfect your comic timing. With all the drama and violence of everyday Roman life, comedies were popular with audiences, especially skits that mimicked minor officials. Romans liked pantomime—a bit like charades. The actors didn't speak, instead using masks and costumes to act out the story, sometimes to music. Only men and boys could take the stage, so boys played the parts of women.

BREAK A LEG...
I ALREADY DID!

Audience
Actors were not the celebrities of today. They were usually foreigners or slaves and they didn't get much respect. A displeased audience could be dangerous!

Actors
Dramatic plays were performed during religious ceremonies and festivals, but with over 200 holidays a year, there were plenty of plays!

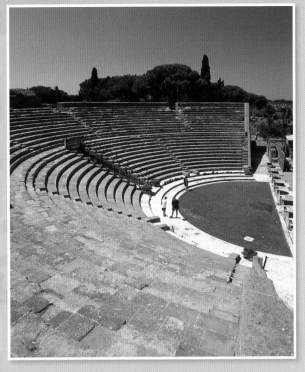

WINNING WAYS

Wealthy nobles would fund performances as a gift to the gods and to the people. This wasn't always an act of generosity— footing the bill for entertainment was a way to increase popularity, power, and respect! They sometimes even paid off members of the audience to react at the right times by snapping their fingers, clapping, and waving a cloth in the air!

Ostia Theater

Amid the ruins of Ostia Antica, ancient Rome's port town, a theater has survived. Historians have worked out it had seating for around 4,000 people. Part of it could be flooded for aquatic performances.

To be or not be in Rome

Rome has built a full-scale reproduction of the Globe Theater in London, where Shakespeare used to perform his plays 400 years ago. It was a gift to the city from a local builder in 2003.

WANT MORE?

The Globe Theater—www.romefile.com/culture/globe-theatre-rome.php

PARK AND GO

Roman drivers don't seem to mind that their cars don't fit. They park anyway! But the crowded streets and seeming lack of road rules in the city drive many visiting drivers to distraction. Many choose to make use of the city's many long-term garages that can be rented by the week. They leave their cars there and set out on foot. Good thinking!

> I HOPE MINE ISN'T ONE OF 500 CARS THAT BREAK DOWN IN ROME EVERY DAY!

On the spot
It's good to know your colors when trying to park—a space with white lines is free, blue lines mean payment is required, and yellow lines mean it's reserved for handicapped drivers.

Local rules?
Lanes don't matter to Rome drivers—as long as they're going in the right direction, they'll happily drift and wander across the road. The strange thing is, it all seems to work.

> STOP LIGHTS? JUST A SUGGESTION!

LIFE CYCLES

Rome is the home of two-wheeled transport—from powerful Ducati and Moto Guzzi sportsbikes, to noisy little "café racers" and, of course, funky Vespas. Rome traffic is so heavy and many of the lanes and alleyways so narrow, that these small scooters are the perfect way to zip about the city.

In the blood
Chariot racing was a huge sport in ancient Rome; its combination of speed and danger thrilled Roman audiences. A similar combination on modern-day Roman roads scares tourists half to death!

SMART MOVERS

Space has always been at a premium in Rome, so it was inevitable that tiny Smart two-seater cars would prove popular there. These short and zippy little vehicles can often be seen parked two or even three to a regular parking spot.

Little beauty!
The original Italian "city car" is the Fiat 500, or Cinquecento, which was manufactured between 1957 and 1975 with a tiny 479cc engine.

WANT MORE?

Driving in Rome :(—www.romebuddy.com/givesadvice/driving.html

STEPPING INTO ROME

Yes, steps are for walking on, but one Colombian man just wouldn't listen. A few years ago he drove his car down the marble steps of the most famous staircase in the world—the Spanish Steps in Rome. He wasn't hurt, but some of the steps were! Despite crazy drivers, tourists still flock to sit and chat on the widest staircase in Europe, although eating on it is now forbidden in an effort to keep the steps clean.

Time to climb

The Spanish Steps were built with French money almost 300 years ago. It's the widest staircase in Europe, and has 138 steps to the top. At the top stands an ancient Roman obelisk and the 16th-century church, Trinità dei Montià.

Church at the top

TOP STUFF!

Santa Maria in Aracoeli is a 6th-century church built on the highest point of the Capitoline Hill, one of the famous seven hills of Rome. Visitors must climb a 124-step staircase to get to it!

A bumpy ride
Thieves in a hurry and confused tourists have been known to use the steps as a road.

Having a ball
In 2008, a prankster tipped half a million brightly colored balls down the steps. The city authorities—who like to keep the area clean and tidy—were not impressed.

STAIRWAY TO HEAVEN

At the Basilica of St. John Lateran in Rome, there is another famous set of steps known as the Holy Staircase. Legend has it that Jesus Christ climbed these steps and that they were brought to Rome from Jerusalem about 1,700 years ago.

WANT MORE?

Every May, the Spanish Steps are decorated with pink azalea flowers. Nice!

BRIDGES OVER THE TIBER

When a river runs through your city, you just build a few bridges to get from one side to the other, right? It wasn't so simple for the Romans. The Tiber flows fast and often flooded. They would just finish building a bridge when a massive surge of water would carry it away. Finally they got with the program and erected massive stone walls on each side to protect the banks.

MORE HELL THAN HEAVEN

It's a beautiful bridge now, but Ponte Sant'Angelo has seen some ugly events. In 1450, almost 200 pilgrims heading to St. Peter's were pushed off the bridge and drowned. Later the bodies of executed criminals were hung from the bridge as a warning!

Ponte Sisto

Built in the mid-1400s by Pope Sixtus IV (which is why it's named Sisto), this footbridge replaced the cable-ferry that used to cross between two of the busiest parts of Rome. The stone used in the Ponte Sisto was taken from the Colosseum.

> DOES THIS LUTE SOUND A LITTLE FLAT TO ANYONE ELSE?

THANKS TO THE TIBER

You only see a bit of it in Rome but the Tiber River runs for over 250 miles (400km), beginning its course on Mt. Fumaiolo and ending at the Tyrrhenian Sea. For the early Romans the river offered a natural highway, allowing ships to bring grain, salt, livestock, and building materials into the city, as well as providing easy access in and out of Rome for the military.

Ponte Sant'Angelo

The bridge was built by Emperor Hadrian 2,000 years ago, but the angel statues were added just 400 years ago to honor an angel who ended the plague.

Ponte Rotto
This leftover bridge, overgrown with weeds and shrubs, is nicknamed the "Broken Bridge." It was first built over 2,000 years ago, but was destroyed by floods. Again and again it was rebuilt, only to be reduced to rubble by the floods. Finally, about 400 years ago, the Romans gave up on it!

Ponte Fabricio
On the oldest bridge in Rome there's a four-faced *herma* of Janus. A what of what? Let's start with Janus. He was a god with two heads, each facing in opposite directions. *Hermai* were stone posts that marked boundaries. A post on the Ponte Fabricio has Janus times two— that's four faces looking out in all directions.

Ponte Cestio
This is the bridge that carries ambulances across the river to Tiber Island, which is home to Fatebenefratelli Hospital.

CLEVER DESIGN
Without computers, the Romans had to work out how to put down foundations that could hold against the force of the water. They came up with a design that was ship-shaped. The pointed end faced the oncoming stream so the water would part when it hit and flow freely and evenly through the segmented arches. Smart huh!

WANT MORE?

Tiber 360° panorama—www.360cities.net/image/the-sant-angelo-bridge-rome

WHAT'S THE BUZZ?

In ancient times the Romans had a large open space called the Forum. If anything happened, the Forum was where you'd hear about it—like an ancient Internet! It was the beating heart of Rome, sitting in what used to be an old marsh between the Capitoline and Palatine hills. It was where issues were debated and decisions were made, and it was the birthplace of the Republic of Rome.

MAKING A POINT

The famous Roman general Julius Caesar met a violent end in the Theatre of Pompey. A bunch of senators were worried that Caesar was about to declare himself the king of Rome, so around 60 of them went after him. He was stabbed 23 times!

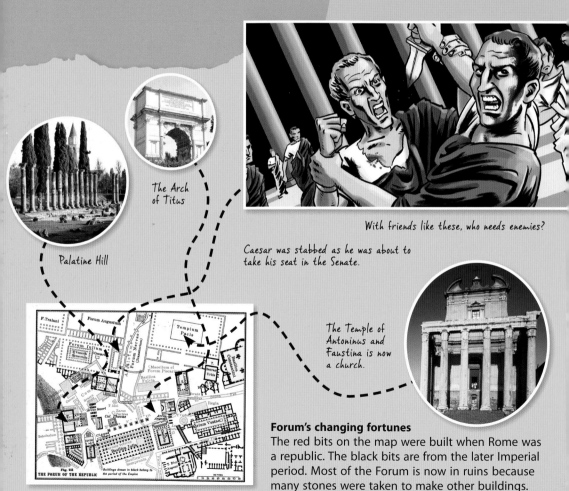

The Arch of Titus

Palatine Hill

With friends like these, who needs enemies?

Caesar was stabbed as he was about to take his seat in the Senate.

The Temple of Antoninus and Faustina is now a church.

Forum's changing fortunes
The red bits on the map were built when Rome was a republic. The black bits are from the later Imperial period. Most of the Forum is now in ruins because many stones were taken to make other buildings.

GUESS WHAT?

ALL TALK!

If you had something to say to the citizens of ancient Rome, you said it at the Forum. There was a tradition of speaking from a platform called the Rostra, which faced the Senate, though many speakers turned their backs on the politicians and addressed the people.

NO WAY!

eaven and earth

here were two separate Senate houses" in the Forum—one was r priests dealing with religious atters, the other was where oliticians debated social issues.

I SHOULD SO PUT THIS UP ON YOUTUBE!

WANT MORE?

The Forum—www.capitolium.org/english.htm

Special delivery
The water flowed gently from a higher level to a lower one. Arches, in one, two, or three tiers, supported the channels across valleys. Tunnels took them through the hills.

Water channels inside

MMM...MELTED SNOW

Eleven aqueducts were built in Rome over a period of about 500 years.

AQUA POWER

The Roman system of waterways, called aqueducts, was incredibly clever. Fresh water from springs and melted snow was directed into tunnels and pipes and transported long distances. Getting fresh water into the cities was part of the reason the Romans ruled an empire!

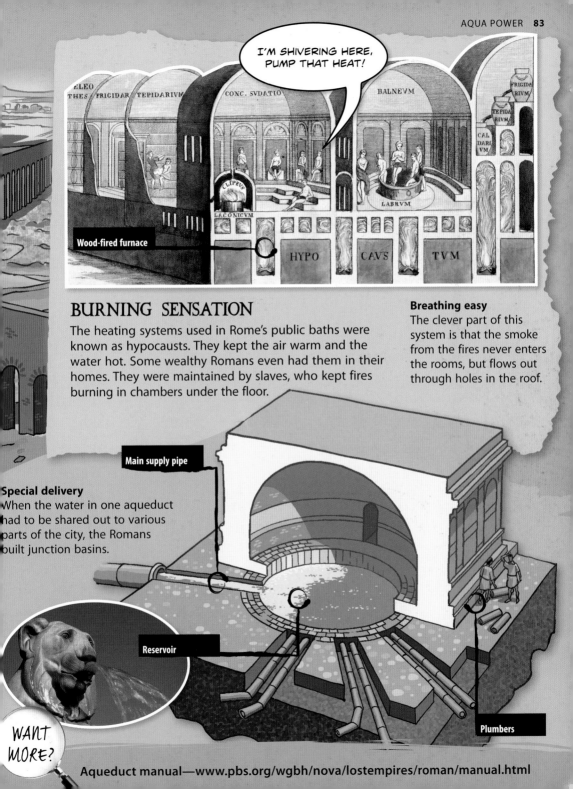

BURNING SENSATION

The heating systems used in Rome's public baths were known as hypocausts. They kept the air warm and the water hot. Some wealthy Romans even had them in their homes. They were maintained by slaves, who kept fires burning in chambers under the floor.

Breathing easy
The clever part of this system is that the smoke from the fires never enters the rooms, but flows out through holes in the roof.

Special delivery
When the water in one aqueduct had to be shared out to various parts of the city, the Romans built junction basins.

Aqueduct manual—www.pbs.org/wgbh/nova/lostempires/roman/manual.html

IT'S ABOUT TIME

Don't bother checking your watch, phone, or computer—you'll know when it's midday in Rome because a cannon is fired! Why? Well, it's dramatic and entertaining, but there's also a historic reason. Before everyone had watches, public clocks were the way to find out the time. Some clocks showed only religious time, dividing the day into six parts according to when prayers were to be said. The boom at midday announced the official time.

A HANDFUL OF HISTORY

★ The cannon is still fired daily, though now from Janiculum Hill.

★ In ancient Rome the length of an hour changed according to the time of year, so an hour was longer in summer than in winter.

★ The day was divided into *ante meridiem* (before midday) and *post meridiem* (after midday.) That's AM and PM!

★ Owning a water clock was a sign of great wealth.

Cannon at the castle
In 1846, Pope Pius IX introduced the custom of firing a cannon at midday from the top of Castel Sant'Angelo. At the sound of the cannon, all the local church bells would ring.

SINE NUBE PLACET

OROLOGIO SOLARE AL TEMPO MEDIO DI ROMA

SERVIBILE DALL'INVERNO ALL'ESTATE

SERVIBILE DALL'ESTATE ALL'INVERNO

DAL 21 DICEMBRE AL 21 GIUGNO

DAL 23 GIUGNO AL 21 DICEMBRE

Here comes the sun
The sundial is the oldest way to measure time. It uses the length of shadows to estimate times of the day. The downside? You need sun to create shadows!

TIME WISE

In 1703, Pope Clement XI decided to build a 150-ft (45-m) long bronze "meridian line" into the floor of the church of Santa Maria degli Angeli. This would be the official time reference for Rome. When it was finished, observers could measure the position of the sun in the sky by watching where the sun's rays fell on the line along a series of notches carved into the floor. The sundial action can still be seen today.

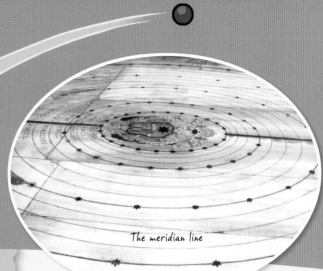

The meridian line

IT'S A HAIR PAST A FRECKLE O'CLOCK

A steady drip, drip, drip...

As well as sundials, the Romans used water clocks. A slow, steady drip of water would gradually fill a container inscribed with marks to record the passage of time. As designs became more inventive, variations included bells that tinkled as water passed each notch and little statues that rose on a float and pointed out the hour.

Italian scientist Galileo invented the pendulum mechanism to keep a clock ticking.

WANT MORE?

The Julian Calendar—www.timeanddate.com/calendar/julian-calendar.html

OW, MY
ACHIN'
BACK!

Michelangelo suffered for art...

Arguing over art

Years after completing the ceiling of the Sistine Chapel, Michelangelo was told to paint the story of the Last Judgment on the altar wall. The Church was furious at his naked figures and campaigned to have the "obscenity" covered.

CHAPEL OF ART

Around 4.5 million people each year visit the Sistine Chapel in the Vatican in Rome. The greatest painters of the time contributed to the religious artwork on the walls and ceiling, including Michelangelo—though some people were so outraged by his naked bodies that fig leaves were later painted over their private parts!

Spark of life

Of all the scenes painted by Michelangelo on the ceiling of the Sistine Chapel, one in particular is often talked about and shown. Called *Creation of Adam*, it depicts a story from the Bible in which God gives the spark of life to Adam, the first man.

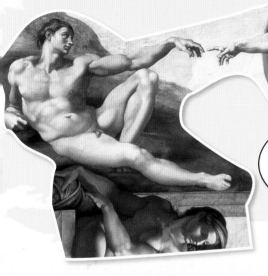

DUDE, YOU'RE MY MAIN MAN. ACTUALLY, YOU'RE THE ONLY MAN!

A HANDFUL OF HISTORY

* ☆ The paintings are *frescoes*, meaning the paint was applied to slightly damp plaster.
* ☆ Michelangelo was told to paint a new ceiling, which didn't thrill him. He preferred to sculpt.
* ☆ The ceiling took four years. He worked on scaffolding, often stuck in odd positions.
* ☆ He painted some 5,000 sq ft (460 sq m) with 300 figures.
* ☆ He was in his sixties when he painted *The Last Judgment*.

Chapel service

The Sistine Chapel isn't just a place for students and tourists to check out amazing artwork. It's also a working chapel where the pope conducts masses and baptisms, and where cardinals gather when it's time to vote for a new pope.

WANT MORE?

The Vatican Museums—mv.vatican.va

WORLD RECORDS

In 1506, Pope Julius II invited the Helvetian soldiers from Switzerland, known for their bravery, devotion, and honesty, to protect Vatican City. Called the Pontifical Swiss Guard, it is the oldest army still in active service—and that's just one of Rome's world records!

OLDEST gallery

Dust off the art

The Capitoline Museums—twin palaces on each side of Piazza del Campidoglio—together hold the record as the oldest public gallery of art in the world.

I DO MORE THAN LOOK GOOD!

OLDEST army in the world

Active duty

These days there's not much call for an army to defend the Vatican, but the Swiss Guard still have a role to play in looking after the safety of the pope.

Record dome in Rome

The domed roof of the Pantheon in Rome is the largest unreinforced concrete dome in the world. No one knows how the Romans did it!

LARGEST unreinforced concrete dome

AMAZING LITTLE VATICAN CITY

In both size and the number of its inhabitants, Vatican City inside Rome is the smallest sovereign state in the world. The population is around 800.

SMALLEST sovereign state

LARGEST church

Largest church in smallest state

St. Peter's Basilica in Vatican City is the world's largest church. It holds 60,000 people!

WANT MORE?

COPPA THAT

Gelato is an Italian style of ice cream, and a place that sells gelato is called a *gelateria*. No matter what flavor you prefer, and whether you order it in a *coppa* (cup) or in a *cono* (cone), there are simple things to know about buying gelato that can make you an instant specialist!

PRODUZIONE PROPRIA

IS IT BAD TO WANT IT ALL?

What's the diff?
Gelato is made with the same sort of ingredients as ice cream, but with less fat. Gelato also has less air than ice cream—some ice creams are half air! And whereas ice cream is served frozen, gelato is served semifrozen, so that it is softer. Because of the differences, the flavors of gelato can be more intense than ice cream.

THE SCOOP ON COLOR

Look for a color that is "real." Too much color means they've added chemicals to make the color stronger. Strawberry should be a pale pink and have little seeds, not be bright pink. Banana should not be bright yellow because that's not how real bananas look.

Granita

Gelaterias also sell granita—crunchy ice crystals that have been flavored, often with fruit. A granita mixture has to be regularly stirred so that the crystals which form on the top go back into the mix.

ARTIGIANALE

Some gelaterias in Rome are over a hundred years old!

Follow the signs

The sign *produzione propria* means the gelato is made on-site, and a sign saying *artigianale* means all-natural ingredients.

WANT MORE?

Gelato recipe—www.ehow.com/how_2058527_make-lemon-gelato.html

Plasmatronic publicity

With a psychedelic snake one moment and rushing rapids the next, an ever-changing plasma screen staircase at Louis Vuitton in Rome draws crowds of tourists and even some serious shoppers.

SHOP TILL YOU DROP

In ancient Rome it was more common to find individual shops—often at the base of apartment blocks or some attached to forums and baths—than to find groups of shops clumped together. Though there are some malls in Rome, the tradition of individual shops continues today.

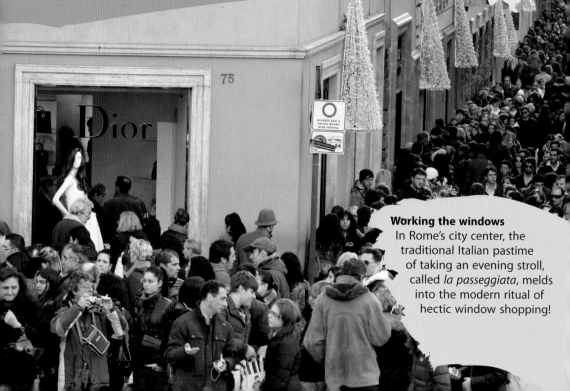

Working the windows

In Rome's city center, the traditional Italian pastime of taking an evening stroll, called *la passeggiata*, melds into the modern ritual of hectic window shopping!

SERIOUS SALES

There's soccer and then there's the shop sales. Romans go crazy for the *saldi*, held officially only twice a year. The government regulates the sales, and there are fines for shopkeepers who break the rules!

> PERFETTO! MEDIUM LIGHTISH DARKISH GREEN.

Shop owners on Via Condotti used to charge customers just to come in and look!

> HAT'S A GOOD START...

BVLGARI

GIANNI VERSACE

DOLCE & GABBANA

Cartier

81

Luxury lane
The main street for glamor shopping is Via Condotti near the Spanish Steps, home to some of the world's most expensive brands.

> WANT MORE?

Trajan Markets (ancient Roman shopping mall)—en.mercatiditraiano.it

INDEX

NOT-FOR-PARENTS
ROME
EVERYTHING YOU EVER WANTED TO KNOW

1st Edition
Published August 2011

Conceived by Weldon Owen in partnership with Lonely Planet
Produced by Weldon Owen Pty Ltd
59–61 Victoria Street, McMahons Point
Sydney NSW 2060, Australia

Copyright © 2011 Weldon Owen Pty Ltd

WELDON OWEN PTY LTD
Managing Director Kay Scarlett
Publisher Corinne Roberts
Creative Director Sue Burk
Senior Vice President,
International Sales Stuart Laurence
Sales Manager, North America Ellen Towell
Administration Manager,
International Sales Kristine Ravn
Managing Editor Averil Moffat
Project Editor Lachlan McLaine
Designer Sarah Taylor - Spicy Broccoli Media
Images Manager Trucie Henderson
Production Director Todd Rechner
Production and Prepress Controller Mike Crowton

Published by
Lonely Planet Publications Pty Ltd ABN 36 005 607 983
90 Maribyrnong St, Footscray, Victoria 3011, Australia

ISBN 978-1-74220-818-3

Printed in Singapore

A WELDON OWEN PRODUCTION

Credits and acknowledgments

Key tcl=top center left; tl=top left; tc=top centre; tcr=top center right; tr=top right; cl=centre left; c=center; cr=center right; bcl=bottom center left; bl=bottom left; bc=bottom center; bcr=bottom center right; br=bottom right; bg=background

20tl, 21tl, 25t, 31br, 35br, 40r, bl, 41cl, b, 62tr, cl, 63tl, 64tr, 66tl, 68cl, bl, 71bg, 85tr, 93b **Alamy**; 18r, 28tl, 57tl, 69c **Bridgeman Art Library**; 9cl, 16bl, 17tr, 21br, 25r, 33br, 42bl, 48cl, b, 49c, bl, 51tr, 54tr, 54-55, 58c, 60tr, bl, 61bl, 64br, 70tr, 72l, 73br, 75bg, br, 77cr, 78r, 79bl, 80c, cl, 81b, 87tl, bl, 88c, 89tl, bl, **Corbis**; 22l, 28tcl, tc, 37tl, 40tr, 43cl, 44c, br, 49tr, 52tr, 55tr, br, 61t, c, tr, 62br, 63c, 64c, 65bg, c, 66tr, 73tl, 74b, 76c, 77bl, 78cl, c, 79tr, 85br, 86tl, 86cr, 88t, tr, 90c, 91b, 92b, 93tl, tr, bl, c, cr **Getty Images**; 8tl, 10c, 11bl, 12cr, 15cl, c, 16cr, 17bl, bg, 18cr, 20-21b, 31cl, 32cr, 33tl, bl, 34br, 36bg, r, 38bl, 42cr, bcr, 43tl, c, 46tl, 47, 49cr, 50tr, 51tl, cl, 53tl, tr, 56cl, c, 56-57b, 57c, cr, 58bl, 59tl, 67tr, cr, 73bc, 82tl, 85cl, **iStockphoto.com**; 14tr, bc, 24tr, 34tl, 39tr, 48cr, 80br, 81tl **Lonely Planet**; 7tr, 9tr, 10-11bg, 19b, 21tr, 23r, 24tl, 19br, 32tl, bl, 33cl, 37bl, 47tl, 51bl, 52b, 59cr, 60br, 69tr, b, 83tr, 92tr **Photolibrary**; 9br **Scala Archive**; 13tl, tr, 14tl, bl, br, 15cl, c, b, 18bl, 19t, 22bl, 22-23, 23tc, 25t, tr, bl, 30cr, 31tr, 33tr, 34cr, 35tr, 39t, 41r, 42tr, l, b, br, 43tr, 44cr, bc, 45t, 47bl, 48bl, 49cl, cr, 50bl, 51br, 54bl, 55tc, 56cr, br, 57cl, 59br, cl, bl, 62br, 66bl, 66-67t, 67b, 68c, 70tl, bl, br, 72br, 75t, cr, 76br, 78bl, 79cr, 82bl, 84br, 86b, bl, 89br, 90r, bl, 91tl, tr, br **Shutterstock**; 12l, 15r, 37r, 51cr, 59tl, 74cr, 80bl **Wikipedia**

All repeated image motifs courtesy of **iStockphoto.com**.

Illustrations

Cover illustrations by Chris Corr

74tr, 75cl, bl, 94tr, bl, 95tcr, 95bc **Chris Corr**; 80cr **Rob Davis/The Art Agency**; 8bl, 24bl, 26l, br, 30-31, 43b, 71c, 76-77t, 82tl, 83br, 84bl **Geraint Ford/the Art Agency**; 7 **Gary Hanna/The Art Agency**; 45b **Adam Hook**; 6bl **Markus Junker/Godd.com**; 6tr, 28bl, 28-29, 38-39 **Malcolm Godwin/Moonrunner Design**; 10bl, 11tr, 23l, 34-35, 73tr **Laurence Porter/KJA-artists**; 12-13b, 46t, b, 47tr, cr, c, bl, 67bl **Francesca D'Ottavi/Wilkinson Studios**; 26-27 **Roger Stewart**; 50c, 53b **Anne Winterbotham**

Maps 49, **Peter Bull Art Studio**

All illustrations and maps copyright 2011 Weldon Owen Pty Ltd.

LONELY PLANET OFFICES

Australia Head Office
Locked Bag 1, Footscray, Victoria 3011
Phone 03 8379 8000 Fax 03 8379 8111
Email talk2us@lonelyplanet.com.au

USA
150 Linden St, Oakland, CA 94607
Phone 510 250 6400 Toll free 800 275 8555 Fax 510 893 8572
Email info@lonelyplanet.com

UK
2nd fl, 186 City Rd, London EC1V 2NT
Phone 020 7106 2100 Fax 020 7106 2101
Email go@lonelyplanet.co.uk